DIVINE
Madness

Divine Madness

Why I'm ^*Still* a Nun

KAROL JACKOWSKI

AVE MARIA PRESS Notre Dame, Indiana 46556

KAROL JACKOWSKI, a member of the Congregation of Holy Cross since 1964, is currently pursuing membership with the Sisters of Christian Community. She lives and works in New York City and is the author of three books, including *Ten Fun Things to Do Before You Die* (Ave Maria Press).

© 1996 by Ave Maria Press, Inc.

Cover and text design: Katherine Robinson Coleman.

Printed and bound in the United States of America.

Library of Congress Cataloging-in-Publication Data
Jackowski, Karol.
Divine madness: why I am still a nun/by Karol Jackowski.

    p.   cm.
ISBN 0-87793-594-7

    1. Monastic and religious life of women.   2. Jackowski, Karol.
    3. Nuns—United States—Biography. I. Title.
BX4210.J33   1996
255'.9—dc20

                                             96-9293
                                             CIP

Contents

The first Day's Night had come—
And grateful that a thing
So terrible—had been endured—
I told my Soul to sing—

She said her Strings were snapt—
Her Bow—to Atoms blown—
And so to mend her—gave me work
Until another Morn—

And then—a Day as huge
As Yesterdays in pairs,
Unrolled its horror in my face—
Until it blocked my eyes—

My Brain—begun to laugh—
I mumbled—like a fool—
And tho' 'tis Years ago—that Day—
My Brain keeps giggling—still.

And Something's odd—within—
That person that I was—
And this One—do not feel the same—
Could it be Madness—this?

Emily Dickinson #410

Introduction

Being a nun was in the beginning, is now, and probably ever shall be the most mysterious fact of my life. Bewitched, bothered, and bewildered am I in trying to make sense of it all, yet rarely does a day go by in which I am not somehow asked to do just that. Living and working as I do with people in New York's East Village—among the world's most counter-cultural residents, my being a nun remains a topic of remarkable interest.

Believer and non-believer, dear friend and stranger, each want to know why I became a nun, or even more so, why I still want to be one. In general, they question why any woman in her right mind would ever want to be a nun, particularly in this day and age when a woman can pretty much be anything she wants. At least I feel I can be anything I want.

For the past few decades the limited few choosing religious life suggest that most right-minded women indeed don't want to be nuns. In 1993, there were nearly 95,000 nuns in the United States compared to an all time high of 180,000 plus in 1966. More specifically, of the fifty of us who entered the Sisters of the Holy Cross in 1964, four celebrated our 25th-year anniversary in 1992. Currently, the average age of nuns in the United States hovers around mid-sixty and is climbing rapidly, leaving a shrinking handful of sisters fortysomething or younger. So since the mid-1960s, some 90,000 women have left the Roman Catholic sisterhood, while nearly 100,000—mostly older—stayed on. Thirty years later, fewer and fewer women in this country consider the sisterhood an attractive life choice. Without a doubt, nuns are quickly becoming an endangered species. Maybe naturally, rightfully, and justifiably so, some would say. I think not.

Enormous changes have taken place in most women's religious communities since the mid-1960's.

Many of us still appear relatively plain and slightly-to-highly out-of-sync with mainstream fashion. Not many nuns like to shop and most tend toward wearing the less noticeable, more serious colors of blue, brown, black, and beige. As family and non-nun friends comment, "Regardless of what you wear, we can spot you in a crowd." On the other hand, many of us no longer look like nuns used to look. And while many nuns still live happily in convents and large groups, some live equally as happily alone in small apartments, or in small groups in ordinary neighborhood houses. In some situations, women who are not nuns, but who associate and work with us, may also live in community with us. Along with the way we dress and witness to religious life, our understanding of community life has also deepened significantly over the past thirty years.

The work we are called to do as nuns—our mission so to speak—has also grown and changed beyond our wildest individual and communal imaginings. Little by little, our work has become more divinely ordinary. While many nuns still choose to educate or nurse in Catholic schools and hospitals, many also pursue the call to serve through a rich and refreshing diversity of works and professions. Joining numerous nurses, teachers, and administrators are lawyers, beauticians, doctors, secretaries, masseuses, social workers, accountants, midwives, artists, bakers, even morticians. Following the call to serve wherever and however people are in need, we sisters have made of ourselves many things to many people. As such we offer different talents, skills, and personalities —but the same creative spirit. The same true God calls to and moves through each and every one. Wherever people are in need, wherever the least among us are found, wherever work is to be done to relieve suffering and protect human dignity, it is not surprising to find sisters—young and old, in and out of habit—living and working at all hours of the day and night.

Yet as sisters become more and more immersed in non-church-related or non-religious-looking work—whether that be teaching in public schools, working in public administration, or entering the ordinary world of the marketplace—the meaning of our unique life becomes more and more obscure. Through the slow but steady stripping away of all those external features which easily defined and set us apart for centuries one big question emerges: If we now live and work and look like everyone else, then why be nuns? Why the sisterhood? What's the difference?

The decision to write about my still wanting to be a nun—even though I now live, work, and look like anyone else—is firmly grounded in the belief that we need never lose faith in our lives as nuns. If we ever lose touch with what attracted and called us in the beginning, if we ever stop listening to our gut instinct, to the still small voice, and ever stop telling one another what we hear, regardless of how disturbing or crazy it may sound, then the mystery that holds us together as nuns in this world will slowly but surely vanish.

One of my greatest inspirations in this regard is the contemplative Carmelite nun, Sister Wendy Beckett, art critic for the BBC. Dressed in full habit, Sister Wendy leaves the cloister, leads us through the world's greatest museums, and talks about the God she finds in art. Within the cloister, Sister Wendy does contemplative work as a writer, authoring several books on the religious experience of art.

Another contemporary inspiration is Sister Helen Prejean, whose work with death-row inmates now moves millions of believers and non-believers alike through her book and the movie based on it, *Dead Man Walking.* And of course there are thousands of unknown sisters whose daily life and work bring inspiration to all those with whom they come in contact. The mystery that binds us together as sisters in this world is simply hearing and following the call of God, wherever and however it leads; it is simply going and telling on the mountain what we hear in the depths of the heart.

In deciding to tell what I hear, regardless of how disturbing or crazy it may sound, I beg the reader not to assume that I speak for all nuns, or for an entire religious community. No individual can be so competent as to speak for all sisters on any or all aspects of religious life. In no way at all does my experience pretend or want to be *a* definition or *the* definition of religious life. It simply represents what has gradually become more clear to me over the past thirtyplus years of my religious life. All parts of this book, therefore, begin, move, and end with one experience in this mysterious world of sisterhood, with one person's attempt to explain what happened and what continues to happen to her there.

From the very beginning in 1964, I understood the call to be a nun in relation to finding out where in the world I do and do not fit, where in the world I do and do not feel altogether at home. While most women grow up called by the pure joy of marriage and/or career, children, money, fame, fashion, and success, I grew up hearing something different. Even though I found none of the above unappealing or unattractive, I repeatedly found myself drawn elsewhere. While I still enjoy thoroughly the pleasure associated with all of the above, in the end I consistently find myself most completely at home somewhere else, usually somewhere more solitary.

The best way I know to describe what happened to me in this strange and mysterious world of religious life is to think first about what society expects of women, then see what I do and do not find in that expectation. Likewise I think as well about what the other world—the world of religious sisters—calls women to be and to do. I've tried to see what I do and sometimes do not find in that call, where I do and sometimes do not fit into the Roman Catholic sisterhood.

While I firmly believe that no life well-chosen and well-lived is any less full of the divine madness I know and love in being a nun, I also believe that the lives of nuns regretfully remain shrouded in a silence that alienates more than it attracts. And if we expect, as I most certainly do, that the very best women will continue to join our life, then it behooves those of us who taste eternal life in this strange land, to tell what we know of the mystery that led us here. We must explain what happened to us, for better or worse, regardless of how inexplicable the experience may feel. The mystery, the divine madness, compels us to tell what we know as does the dark uncertainty of the future.

Whether we are now witnessing the historic, natural death of Catholic women's religious communities or the natural rebirth of communities of seemingly madwomen destined to renew the face of the earth, I believe depends upon returning to the beginning. In the beginning lies the mystery which calls women to sisterhood and works of mercy. This is the mystery that moves us through the best and worst of times, the mystery that leads us into a future far beyond our wildest imaginings.

My greatest hope in all of this is that women who may now experience similar mysteries moving in and through their lives, will be seriously encouraged to consider joining such a life. Even though the secular world continues to minimize everything about women except their ability to be attractive and submissive, certainly women have not altogether lost soul, the supernatural instinct we have for a life which is nothing less than divine. Certainly those gods and goddesses, who for millennia have been calling women to divine life in religious communities, have not, all of a sudden, lost interest in such sisterhood. And most certainly, they have not, all of a sudden, lost their voice.

ONE

The Call

What at first felt like a mysterious invitation from God to become a nun, over the years grew into a magnificent obsession regarding all things religious, all things extraordinary, all things divine. It now feels as though I have always been fascinated with the mysterious, with what ordinary people hold sacred, with how people think of and search for God, with the kinds of rituals we create, and with what we do to get in touch with God. It's as though this magnificent God-given obsession with the inner life, with the mysterious workings of the heart and soul, came together like a quite natural response to what I have somehow always known and experienced as "the call."

I was born and raised Catholic at a time when Catholicism overflowed with all manner of things religious, mysterious, and extraordinary.

Everything I remember about my early religious life centers not only around family and friends, but also around the time spent in Catholic schools. Nearly 75% of my childhood was spent in Catholic schools and churches with their larger-than-life reminders of the presence of God and the company of angels and saints. Above the chalkboard in every classroom hung a crucifix which we saluted every morning along with the American flag. And throughout every dark classroom hallway stood statues of angels and saints.

Nearly every day at Saint Stanislaus School in East Chicago, Indiana, nuns told and retold in great detail stories of the lives of saints, incredible and miraculous stories of ordinary people who experienced unthinkable torture and death because of their brave belief and daring determination to follow the call of God. So profound was the impact of those stories, that I can still remember far more vividly the goriest details of each saint's death than the saintly significance of their lives.

As important as these stories were, Christian Doctrine was always the first and most important subject we studied. "Growth in Religious Habits" topped the conduct side of the report cards indicating its equal importance. "Participating in religious activities," "being reverent in prayer and in church," "practicing self control," and "obeying promptly and willingly," were just as important as were reading, writing, and math.

In addition to textbooks and uniforms, we received blessed rosary beads, prayerbooks, daily missals, and holy cards picturing a saint on the front and a wish-come-true prayer on the back. Nearly every year we received a card which made us think and pray for a vocation, for "the call" to become a nun or priest. Even in the Catholic grade school world of holy card trading (which we did then in the 1950's like my nephews do with sports cards now), the vocation card had no trade value whatsoever. Seems like no one wanted the call or the card. Nonetheless, most of us wore medals and scapulars, or carried some religious token (or kept one hidden in a secret place) believing in its divine mysterious power to protect us from harm or to grant our wishes.

From all over the world we received news of extraordinary events. In Turin, Italy, a burial cloth believed to be imprinted with the crucified body of Jesus, was revered. Only a generation before, the Mother of God appeared to children my age at Fatima in Portugal, giving them messages from her Son.

On the local level, we experienced our own intensely personal and mysterious firsts—first confession and holy communion—as well as all the mysterious specials such as benedictions, May crownings, living rosaries, novenas, and a personal favorite, forty hours devotion.

In the beginning, nuns appeared as the caretakers and preservers of God's mysteries, as well as God's house. This roving band of women, clearly not of this world, attended to God's work wherever they went. For all eight of my Catholic grade school years I was taught and befriended by these women, these Sisters of Saint Joseph. Every day began with what we then understood as the Holy Sacrifice of the Mass. Candles flickered, incense burned and rose. In mysterious Latin we sang Gregorian chant and heard the words by which ordinary bread and wine where changed into the Body and Blood of Christ. All of this moved me to listen for messages from God. And now, only in a somewhat different manner, all of this continues to move me to do the same.

There is not now, nor has there ever been anything unusually dramatic or noteworthy about the call I hear—no visible appearances of the Mother of God with envelopes containing messages from her Son. No extraordinary signs, stories, afflictions, or miracles. Nor did I come from a strict, religiously observant family that always prayed and wished for one of its five children to become a nun or priest. Quite the contrary, thank God. The manner of the call I hear has always been altogether ordinary, even though the life it calls me to appears bizarre and extraordinary to the majority who hear a quite different call.

In the beginning, I found the call so vague and obscure that I could not, would not, identify it as an invitation from God to become a nun. In the very beginning I didn't feel called by anyone to become anything in particular.

The only calls I ever remember hearing in my early years were those of my dear father to work in the Normal Bakery, our family-owned business, and occasionally to go fishing on Sunday mornings. Or those calls of my dear mother to clean my room, turn down the stereo, get off the phone. Or, most important of all, the calls of my friends to come out and play.

All I know now about the mysterious beginning of my religious life is that I recognized the call simply as a voice—a still, small, inner voice—a kind of hunch, an intuitive gut-instinct. It told me what to do and where to go, like a divining rod showing my thirsty soul where to find water. For years this divining rod did not lead me to do anything that set me apart from the life and fun I knew with family and friends. From all outward appearances, nothing in my early life indicated I was in any way destined to enter the convent. Friends, fun, and family were far too important, and from what I could see then, far too absent from religious life for me to even consider becoming a nun. As a matter of fact, if there were such a class award at the time, I surely would've been voted "Least Likely..." by my classmates.

All I know now about the very beginning of the call is that, little by little, I discovered I had a mind, a voice of my own, and another mind—as though my mind also had a mind of its own with a more thoughtful, insightful voice. Early on I learned to let my conscience be my guide. I did not feel guided in any real or imagined way to become a nun, or for that matter, to do anything else dramatically different with my life. In the beginning my life felt like one great big blank to be filled in and I liked it that way a lot.

While the instinct about what to do with one's life may not at first be fully developed, as mine surely was not, the need to play and roam around until we find what we need is always ripe and ready. This is a good instinct, a most divine experience, even if it eventually leads to mistakes. Even through the most impressive mistakes, instincts become refined and conscience becomes sharper, eventually guiding us to other insights, leading us to even better and brighter choices.

I don't see mistakes when I look back at how I followed the call as much as I see turning points, times when I naturally turned from the only life I knew and loved in search of something more. It was as though something were missing and had to be found. At times all of my experiences called and led me elsewhere, oftentimes somewhere more solitary, more mysterious and serious, and more inexplicable. For me, then as well as now, strangely and surprisingly, such head-turning experiences also proved to be far more interesting and fun, and in that way far more divine.

One such turning point occurred sometime during my junior and senior years of high school, when life suddenly demands an unprecedented seriousness—a decision about what to do after graduation. A strange, new, inner obligation appeared then, a need to start becoming whoever and whatever I was meant to be, to follow whatever offered the greatest chance for me to be and do my very best. For those of us who were high-spirited and paid far more attention to social life than the inner life, this was a time of great awakenings and great expectations. It was time to take the first steps toward a future of our own making, a life of our own design. The vagueness and obscurity which characterized the call I knew in the beginning now begged for some measure of clarity.

While my nearest and dearest friends began visiting colleges, looking for jobs, or planning their weddings, I found myself strangely, secretly, and uncharacteristically attracted to and fascinated by the work and the life of the nuns who taught me in high school, the Sisters of the Holy Cross. They awakened and valued as divine the creative life of my mind and the love I had for theater and writing thereby turning my life in directions new but true to me, and completely beyond my adolescent understanding.

While the lives of nuns then were more shrouded in secrecy and silence than now, I found myself attracted to what I saw as smart, independent, funny, mysterious women, singleheartedly intent on doing good and brave works of mercy. Through their excellence in teaching, these strange women cultivated and cared for the way we lived our lives, for what we teenagers held sacred, and for the then wild and crazy ways in which we sought to experience the fullness of life.

All I really, truly knew at that time was this surprising need, this growing, intensifying impulse to follow my uninformed, naive fascination with the strange life and work of these women, to yield to its mysteriousness, even leave family and friends for the sake of it. I vaguely knew that anything which stirs us that differently and deeply, which moves us to the point of distraction and urgently invites us to follow, must always be held sacred. It must be respected, taken seriously, never minimized, or regarded as foolishness. In the beginning I believed and trusted but now I know for sure, that such is the way of God.

Because my attraction to religious life felt so eccentric, so impulsive, and so unlike anything family and friends expected of me, I mostly found myself tightly wrapped in silence, unable to talk to dear family or best friends about what I felt called to do with my life. As a matter of fact, I informed my family of the decision to become a nun through a letter sent in the U.S. mail. A letter was all I could squeeze out of what felt like a profound and absolute speechlessness. Best friends found out about my entering the convent at a New Year's Eve slumber party. There we were, young women under the influence, revealing deep, dark, don't-ever-tell-anyone secrets, those pure teenage best-friend secrets that get passed along, again in secret, the very next day.

In retrospect, I see how my dumb-feeling speechlessness was due largely to the fact that I knew of no one else having experiences similar to mine. Everything I experienced then felt entirely inexplicable. It wouldn't tolerate exposure. As Rainer Maria Rilke explained in his *Letter to a Young Poet*:

> "…something new has entered us, something unknown; our feelings grow mute in shy embarrassment, everything in us withdraws, a silence rises, and the new experience, which no one knows, stands in the midst of it all and says nothing."

That's exactly how I felt in the beginning. Consequently, like Emily Dickinson whose birthday I love sharing, I literally felt like "I needed more veil." And like the reclusive poet, the consequence of this mysterious need for "more veil" was a kind of extreme but by no means terrible loneliness. What I knew then was more of an oddly peaceful and calming sense of having to let myself be carried along by the current of this strange attraction, this mysterious call, this odd decision, without a clue where it would take me or why.

I delayed as long as I could taking any formal steps toward entering the convent, believing maybe it would pass in favor of some more normal life choice. All I found in the delay was that the time had really, truly come for me to follow those sisterly women with whom I felt such a strong, irresistible affinity. The time had come to take my life to a place where support and understanding might be found for my strange, inexplicable experiences. I'm still not sure how or why, but the time had clearly come in the summer of 1964, at the young age of eighteen, to close my eyes, hold my nose, and jump into what always feels like a massive cloud of unknowing.

I was accepted by the Sisters of the Holy Cross on July 13, 1964, the feast of Saint Henry (whose name my father, brother, and nephew share), and left home for the convent exactly two months later.

Both then and now, I've known a vague sense of destiny experienced as divine with this oddly irresistible attraction to a life in a religious community. It's as if this life as a nun, ridiculous though it may sound, is altogether God's idea, designed for me in the stars, or in the words of the 139th Psalm "formed in my inmost being and knit while in my mother's womb." This sense of divine destiny, this strange experience of a "call from God," carries with it the inner security, strength, and peace of mind I need to go my own way, regardless of what critics have to say. It also bears with it the most comforting of blessings—the only kind of courage we ever need—that of facing and accepting life's strangest, most mysterious, most inexplicable experiences as divine, of greeting each new twist and turn in life with utmost respect.

So strong was the experience of being called to vowed religious life at the time, that I remember not being able to envision myself doing any other thing, or living any other way. Any thoughts to do so, even now, bring a noticeable loss of energy, an inner numbness, that reminds me of how those sins against the Holy Spirit must feel, those sins Jesus calls "unforgivable." I know now with far greater clarity what I somewhat blindly believed in the very beginning of my religious life. The inner voice I hear calling me to be a nun comes from a most Holy Spirit indeed, the Holiest Spirit I know, an image, an experience of God which mysteriously cannot and clearly will not be denied. Over and over, something altogether spiritual calls, shows next steps, and almost always leaves me feeling as though I end up exactly where I belong, doing exactly what I should be doing. Like some kind of divine inner necessity, the call always waits patiently, enduringly, to be heard, slowly but surely taking me where I gladly would and sometimes sadly would rather not go.

Years ago, I found enormous comfort in something Carl Jung wrote about fearing this most Holy Spirit. He claimed good reason for such fear, not because the spirit wanted to hurt us, but because of how extremist and radical the Holy Spirit can be when it comes to living a religious life. From the very beginning, nothing appeared more extremist and revolutionary to me than being a nun. Nothing appeared further removed from the life I lived and loved, and nothing felt scarier. In the words of Sister Madeleva, the renowned Holy Cross sister whose vocation pamphlet I was given as a gift, I often feared and dreaded that I was "One Girl in a Hundred, who did not even want to think of a religious vocation for fear that God would catch her in the act and impose a vocation upon her."

Even when the call became clear enough to recognize, even when I knew I was mysteriously slipped the nun card and had to deal with it, I had no idea whatsoever what being a nun meant, or what I had to go through in order to become one.

In the beginning of my religious life I knew absolutely nothing at all about what went on beyond convent walls. Nor did anyone else, it seemed, but nuns themselves, and a handful of priests. No one ever talked about what nuns did at home, or what a day in the life of a nun was like. In the very beginning, I clearly knew not what I was doing, but then again, neither did the other forty-nine new sisters who entered the convent with me.

There was and still is to a degree, a kind of holy secrecy about the life of a nun, its rites of initiation and its rituals. It is not a repressive, censoring, or clandestine secrecy, but rather a protective, preserving, careful secrecy. Its holy role is still that of guarding as divine the mysteries around which the lives of nuns are built. Traditionally the mysteries are those of poverty, celibacy, and obedience. Personally, I know the mysteries of sisterhood as solitude, work, and madness; as a divinely mad way of life whose gate appears far too narrow and whose manner appears far too eccentric to most.

In the beginning, out of that great big, silent mystery of being a nun, it was the sisterhood, the solitude, the work, and the madness of the nuns that first called me to follow. Yet all that was evident in the beginning of the call was the sheer eccentricity of my decision, the good joke I was taking too far, the big bets that I'd be home in six weeks. To many it appeared as though my decision to become a nun was solely reflective of my own particular kind of adolescent madness. Admittedly so, even in the very beginning, the madness of it all strangely and strongly appealed to me. Even now, I still like the idea of living way out there on the fringe, on the edge of society, in that solitary margin, where all things mysterious happen.

Even in the very beginning, the sheer madness of being a nun held a divine appeal all its own. The strange, hidden, mysterious otherworld in which nuns lived was one in which I, for reasons not at all clear to me, wanted to live also. Sisterhood, solitude, work, and madness appeared the less traveled roads, each taking me in a different direction then and now. And each still offers a very good reason why any woman would ever want to be a nun.

TWO

Sisterhood

Of all the ways I can relate to others, dear friend as well as near stranger, I am most attracted to and most at home with doing so as sister and in association with other women who also hear the call to sisterhood, and the divine life it offers. What I still find most enchanting about the call is how important, even holy, it regards a woman's need to get together regularly with other women.

It's as though the call to sisterhood lies secretly buried within the soul of all women, always longing and waiting to be heard. Even though most women do not seek to live sisterhood in religious life, getting together regularly somehow answers that call. So important is such getting together among women that it becomes a heartfelt ritual, a mysterious rite of sisterhood to be nourished and protected for generations to come.

Way before I even noticed the sisterhood of nuns, I loved my mother's monthly Girls Night Out with eleven other women who called themselves the *Chere Amies,* the Dear Friends. With the exception of December, when the *Chere Amies* had their Christmas get-together with husbands for an evening of dinner and dance, they always took turns meeting at one another's houses for a night of food, drink, and cards—usually pinochle or bunko. Prizes were valued at $3.00, $2.00, and $1.50. They paid monthly dues—with which they occasionally went out to lunch—picked the gardenia as the club flower, "Doodlee-Doo" as the club song, and planned a picnic at the lake each summer for all the *Chere Amies* families.

While the husbands and children of the *Chere Amies* were not allowed at the monthly get-togethers, I still remember sneaking as close as I could without being seen, straining to hear what they talked about that provoked such hearty laughter, unendingly into the night. I remember late-night laughter more than anything else and still envy whatever it was that made these dear friends laugh so hard and so long, as though they held it in and waited all month to do so. Between club meetings, they talked frequently on the phone, filling each other in on the days of their lives. Those who lived near one another—like my mother, Shirley, and her best friend, Estelle Nowosinski—often got together for a cigarette and coffee-talk after getting all their children off to school. They also called each other *dollka,* a Polish term of endearment between girlfriends, and referred to their daughters as "little *dollkas.*" We were all *dollkas* then, and we still refer to one another that way now.

Not only did the *Chere Amies* celebrate births, weddings, and successes of each other's family members, they also came together to offer comfort, support, and meals-on-wheels in the event of sickness or death. Such was the sisterhood among the *Chere Amies,* such was the friendship among these women that they became family to one another in the ways that matter most. Out of the *Chere Amies* mysteriously grew this whole gathering of family, drawn and held together by the lifeblood of friendship, the kind of lifeblood I imagined I'd find in religious.

Three *Chere Amies* survive at this writing, my mother among them. All three continue to get together on occasion, though the monthly get-togethers are long gone. So important and so indestructible is the sisterly bond among these women that I cannot help but see their friendship as one of the earliest seeds of sisterhood sown in my soul.

Practically every woman I know tells similar stories of clubs to which their mothers belonged. Practically every woman I know also tells stories of similar groups to which they belong, groups which cultivate true loyalty and enduring bonds of trust, as well as the best and most hilarious of times. In retrospect, I understand this longing to get together with our own kind as a primal instinct among women. A level of comfort is found and the affinity of soulmates sometimes develops.

Such groups often form out of some shared experience, and at some particularly moving time in one's life. For example, the *Chere Amies* came together in war years, when part of each meeting was spent putting together packages and writing letters to their soldier husbands, as well as supporting one another.

My sister Debbie gets together with three other women one Friday night a month to play Scrabble. They came together originally because no one in their own families wanted to play Scrabble. Another group of women I know, called The Secret Order of Judith, met weekly for years to survive better an inordinately bullish, boorish, and oppressive boss. Even though these Judys—as they refer to themselves—are now scattered all over the country, the bonds of sisterhood remain. Mini-reunions still occur, at least annually.

Right now, in a kind of auxiliary sisterhood, three of us, two artist friends and myself, literally rearrange our lives every Friday night in order to get together to watch a favorite TV show *(The X-Files)* and to discuss all the otherworldly truths out there in which we wholeheartedly believe. Such are the ordinary mysterious ties that continue to bind women together in sisterhood, and such is the sisterhood by which I still love being bound.

In the beginning, in the very beginning, I always imagined nuns as glorified *Chere Amies*, a society of dear friends whose mysterious purpose was to do God's work the way Jesus did. I saw a community of sisters whose lives were bound together in such a way as to enhance and hold sacred the life and work of women. From what I could see among the nuns I knew, the bonds of sisterhood were believed to be friendships of the most important kind, so much so that nuns regarded the closeness between sisters as holy, as one of the most divine experiences offered to women. The ties of sisterhood that bound the nuns I knew appeared to me as something by which I also wanted to be bound. It was a way of life and a kind of friendship that I found mysteriously attractive.

The very first thing I noticed about the sisterhood of nuns was how all were treated as equal. The sisters who cooked and cleaned and did laundry were valued members of the community just as much as the sisters who ran the schools or administered hospitals. Members formed only one class.

All enjoy the same rights and privileges. I liked that a lot. And even though a few sisters were given the title of Superior, and one the title of Superior General, or Mother Superior, nuns in general didn't seem to care at all about who made the most money, had the most prestigious job, was the smartest, skinniest, or most attractive. The sisterhood of religious women appeared to take clear and consistent exception to all the ways the world calls women to be inordinately competitive and preoccupied with outdoing one another.

Among the nuns I knew, each sister seemed to be a spiritual treasure, a pearl of great price oftentimes, with the very least among them in the eyes of this world being the most loved. It was this equality that most attracted me in the beginning.

For nuns, it always seemed like it's only what's inside a person that really counted. In that inner world we all bear a most divine self, an image and an experience of God unlike that of anyone else. Based on that simple truth, nuns behold all women as holy, as sources of divine life. They consequently work to build community free from any kind of racial or cultural exclusiveness, communities nourished by the divine life of equality, by a new and better social order, a far better and truer way for women to behold themselves and one another.

I think it's partly as a result of this divine equality among sisters that their time together—whether for prayer, for food, for study, or for fun—was always regarded as holy time. Every aspect of our daily lives, no matter how mundane, provided an opportunity for some divine experience, for the cultivation and development of those lifelong bonds of trust and devotion, and for the simple joy of resting in the pure pleasure of one another's company.

Some of my earliest and warmest memories of sisterhood are precisely of such times, particularly during the formative years as a new nun, where any difficulty I experienced in the sudden and dramatic separation from family and friends was made altogether bearable by the heartwarming and often hilarious company of my sisters, my *chere amies.*

Researchers now report similar bonds of sisterhood being formed among women who attend all women's colleges—those rare, supportive, lifelong bonds that form in that environment. Having spent nearly all of my adult life in both environments, the sisterhood of nuns, and the sisterhood of a residential women's college, I've known a lifetime of nurturing of those first seeds of sisterhood reminiscent of those scattered by the *Chere Amies.*

I understand far more clearly now what I very vaguely felt in the beginning. Through the interweaving of all those funny, bizarre, angry, joyful, and painful memories the soul of sisterhood is born. Living under one roof together for extended periods causes a kind of mysterious emotional gluing to take place, one to the other, sister to sister to sister, in ways that would probably not happen otherwise. I can see more clearly now how that's the sacred stuff the sisterhood of religious is made of, that divine richness of interwoven experience, memory, and heartfelt belief in God.

In the very beginning of my religious life, I experienced what I always knew with family and friends, but feared I might not find in the convent. I encountered that divine stuff, the pure fun, the belonging, and the creative energy that flows freely from our singular kind of soulfulness. Being surrounded by sisters, dear friends who wholeheartedly supported, encouraged, and literally applauded one another's creative instincts, was something I had grown accustomed to at home. Because I experienced such support to be as essential as the air that I breathe, I was enormously relieved to find the same among my new sisters in the convent. With heartfelt warmth I remember those sisters who surrounded me in the beginning, who picked up where family and friends left off, making me feel altogether at home in what at first felt like such a strange new world.

More than anything it was this sisterhood— the women religious with whom I shared those first few years of solitary life—that helped me see most clearly who I really was. It helped me find out all the things I was meant to be: high school teacher, counselor, administrator, campus minister, residence hall director, and college dean.

Having passed through all of the nun initiation rites together with those sisters, I discovered my very best self with them, including the early prophetic glimpses of my current self, the solitary writing one. Just as family and friends had done once, life with the sisters continued to connect me further and deeper to the realm of loving, caring, and enjoying, to the depths of my own solitary heart, to the still small voice of my own mostly silent soul. And in helping connect me to my best and truest self, to all the creative spirits stirring within, those sisters connected me to them in ways that neither time nor distance can alter.

Quite clearly, the friendships I know in this sisterhood bear a mysterious quality, an affectionate attachment free of emotional knots, that became a critical support system for me almost instantly. It continues to amaze me that what happens to one sister is felt in some way by all. The joys and sorrows of one are shared in very much the same way as happens in healthy families where members love one another "constantly from the heart" (1 Peter 1:22). Because of those deeply rooted, lifelong friendships, those first strong ties of sisterhood that still sweetly bind, a divine energy is somehow made available, mostly when least expected. It lifts us up and carries us through those life experiences that may appear inordinately difficult and insurmountable.

I recently experienced a remarkably speedy recovery from surgery through what my doctor referred to as "unusual healing powers." Such remarkable experiences, I believe, get their wings from the prayerful power of sisterhood, the tender loving care of family, sisters, and friends, as well as the "unusual healing powers" of an exceptional physician and surgeon. This is the sacrament of sisterhood in my life, all part of the ordinary power of sisterhood's mysterious ties. After years and years of such prayerful, powerful sisterhood, I cannot help but believe that the very same "unusual healing powers" are not available to everyone. Not everyone is like the sisters I know and love, both in and out of the convent, who revere as sacred and regard as holy, the life and friendship of women.

Even while exclusive friendships with emotional knots are always discouraged within the sisterhood of vowed religious, the divine importance of friendship prevailed as essential to the formation and development of any sort of enjoyable community life. Such bonds of friendship still serve as a buffer, a simple and soulful protection, against the more institutional forces of religious life which insist on paying continual and particular attention to uniformity, recognized in the old nun rule book as "the natural guardian of order and union."

When it comes to the notion of uniformity in a religious community, to being made into the image and likeness of a nun, I have been in the more traditional eyes of some, a "poor fit." Even when we all looked the same, followed the same schedule, and were taught to believe the same things, I nearly always felt and was perceived by others as marginal. I was a card-carrying member but in no way mainstream.

"Lack of religious decorum," was a frequent criticism direct toward many of us, myself included. That meant our behavior—the way we laughed, walked, talked, even thought—was judged inappropriate for a nun and needed to be changed.

According to the rule book, in those days, nuns were "...to conduct themselves with becoming gravity, avoiding in speech and action all frivolity and whatever may attract undo attention." In the very beginning that pretty much felt like it covered my whole life. And so disruptive was I to the silence with which we were expected to do our "obediences,"—our household tasks—that I was once given the solitary job of pulling the weeds out of the cracks in the sidewalk out front, and scrubbing the bird droppings off the picnic tables out back. The blessing in disguise was found in being outside, which I could never get enough of. The curse, however, lay in the fact of how inordinately intense that midwestern sun was to one literally dressed from head to foot in layers of black wool.

Being a poor institutional fit was and still is no great burden for me mostly because I'm certainly never alone in that regard. Also the sisters with whom I lived and worked, in the same Holy Spirit as that of my family and friends, accepted, loved, and enjoyed me all the same. I always believed, and still do, that one of the finest and most interesting features of the sisterhood is its rather high percentage of women who are "poor fits" in one way or another. One particular favorite of mine was an old, sometimes sweet, sometimes surly, Irish nun, who usually sat next to me in the back of the community room where we gathered for house meetings. Nearly sixty of us were living together at the time, this being the 1970s and the dawn of group participation. As a result, house meetings ended up both way too big and way too long.

At the beginning of every year, usually in September, elections topped the house meeting agenda. Several sisters were elected to help the superior manage house business—grocery shopping, car maintenance, finances. Paper ballots were passed out, sisters were nominated, and those with the most votes became finalists. I remember how every year, for nearly ten years, this old Irish nun would glance up and down over the list, nod her head, then turn to me and whisper quite loudly, "You're very smart. You do just what I do. You live your life in such a way that no one in their right mind would vote for you." As funny as it was, it was quite true. I never wanted votes, either in or out of the convent, surely the hallmark of an institutional misfit.

The inclination toward uniformity in religious community, toward building up and glorifying the mainstream nun is, I find, one of the more mindless trappings of wanting to treat all nuns as equal. A big part of being treated as equal rests on the common belief that what binds people together is infinitely more important, superior, and holy than what distinguishes them as divine. Commonalities tend to be recognized, treasured, and rewarded far more so than differences. This usually makes equality far less of a blessing than a curse, even for those in the mainstream.

Sometime in the late 1970s, I was awakened by a phone call from the sister who operated the college switchboard asking if I could come up to her office as soon as possible. At the time, I was working as a residence hall director and assumed the call was related to some student prank. With nearly the entire switchboard flashing on "hold," she stood up and asked if I noticed anything different. After I wrongly guessed that she had gotten a new outfit—she was always fashionably dressed—she pointed to her ears which were pierced with those tiny gold starter-studs. Before I could comment on how good they looked, she said, "Why don't you get yours pierced too?" The truth of the matter was revealed when I asked why and she confessed, "Because at breakfast all the nuns were saying, 'God, not even Karol has her ears pierced!'"

I learned two big lessons in religious life that morning: one, even superficial differences weren't easily tolerated in the sisterhood; and two, I had somehow become a measure by which eccentric nun behavior was determined. I might also ironically add that now, some twenty years later, many nuns sport pierced ears, but true to form, I am not one of them.

Moving with the mainstream and preserving the status quo remain forces to contend with. But within women's religious communities, there are other more powerfully positive forces stirring, movements that comfort, protect, and sustain, solidarity that arises from those deeply rooted friendships that hold sisterhood together. Acting because of and with friends is always a powerful, sustaining force. It endows each individual with a rare, mysterious strength that oddly comes with numbers, an inexhaustible energy to work tirelessly for justice in this increasingly and excessively unjust world. Every work that every sister does, whether in the impoverished countryside of Bangladesh, or in the wealthiest suburbs of Washington D.C., bears the loving, moral, and prayerful support of such sisterhood. As a result, a kind of corporate identity emerges, that of "Sister," whereby each and every work of each and every sister bears witness to something far greater than she alone. By virtue of her identity as "Sister," each lives in such a way that above all bears witness to the other-worldliness of sisterhood, to the divine life within us all, and to the loving and merciful works of Christ.

Other than the lifeblood support of family and friends, I can imagine nothing more loving and uplifting than the mysterious corporate support which keeps sisterhood alive. In a heartfelt way we stand behind one another and with one another during the best and worst of times. I cannot imagine anything more devastating and deadening than the absence or withdrawal of such strong, sisterly support. So divine and universal is the solidarity I now find among many sisters that what once was for "nuns only" has slowly been transformed into a sisterhood of everywoman, where any woman, in particular the very least among us, is as warmly welcomed, received, and accepted as any other nun.

It is not at all unusual now to find sisters, living alone or together, working among the most abused, the homeless, the marginal, the heartbroken and rejected of women, with the very least among us in every corner of the world because there we behold the face of God as Mother and as Sister. There, painfully, divine life is found and revered. Such is the divine solidarity that now calls and binds all women, all sisters, together. Such it is, I believe, that keeps the mysterious call to sisterhood alive.

Not only did I hear the friendship and the solidarity of sisterhood of religious women call me in the beginning, but I also simultaneously found myself attracted to the community life nuns built, to the way in which they organized their lives around the mystery of sisterhood.

In the beginning, all I knew about community life was that nuns spent a lot of time together, a lot of time alone, and other than their simple clothes, owned little else. This all appealed to me in some inexplicable way. It still appeals to me, only much more understandably so. From what I recall of the very beginning, the formula for community life simply involved everyone doing everything together at the same time, with little deviation, day after day, for years.

Oddly enough, I remember little detail of those early years as a nun, except for the funniest moments, leading me to believe that there were no distinguishing events that occurred during that time. Or perhaps part of me was in such primal shock as to be rendered unconscious and incapable of remembering. While the truth of the matter probably lies in a bit of both, it's the monotony of days that has the strangest effect on memory, days that all looked something like this:

5:00 a.m.	Rising Bell
5:30 a.m.	Lauds *(Morning Prayer)*
6:00 a.m.	Mass
7:00 a.m.	Breakfast *(In Silence)*
8:00 a.m.	Housework *(In Relative Silence)*
9:00 a.m.	Class / Study / Private Prayer
11:45 a.m.	Examination of Conscience *(Midday Prayer)*
12:00 p.m.	Lunch *(Usually in Silence)*
12:45 p.m.	Recreation

1:30 p.m.	Class / Study / Private
5:00 p.m.	Prayer Vespers *(Evening Prayer)*
6:00 p.m.	Dinner *(Part Silence / Part Talking)*
6:45 p.m.	Recreation
7:30 p.m.	Compline *(Night Prayer)*
8:00 p.m.	Grand Silence
9:00 p.m.	Lights Out

Given the singular similarity of those days, and even though so much of the day was spent in relative silence, the surprising advantage of everyone doing everything together at the same time clearly was found in how well we got to know each other. For example, in the novitiate, when one sister in the dorm lay awake with a nagging cough, or silently sobbed over some unspoken anguish, we all tossed and turned through the night. We all walked around with puffy, sleepless eyes the next day. Likewise, when something terribly funny happened at a most serious time, even the most innocent and devout was forced to stifle a side-splitting laugh. Within the context of all this constant togetherness the best and worst of ourselves was revealed, accepted, and embraced. And in the beginning, all of that constant togetherness took on a most profound importance, as though surviving its intensity was some kind of holy rite of initiation into sisterhood, some sort of blessed boot-camp that would bind us together forever.

For nearly twenty years I lived happily in community groups of anywhere from six to sixty members, befriending, I believe, some of the very best sisters a woman can ever hope to find. Each bore a richness of experience and a wisdom of age that remains with me now, even years after their deaths. I carry timeless gifts from this band of angels who watch over me, lead the way, lift me up, and cheer me on. In a way that only age and sisterhood can fashion, these women remain among the funniest and most interesting I know. Not only did these sisters spin the best tales of life in the religious community, but they also bestowed upon me their own mysterious fearlessness and peace of mind about having to go their own way, regardless of what critics had to say. When I look back especially at those formative years of living and doing everything together under one roof, I can see it was there, divinely and mysteriously there, that the blessed bonds of sisterhood grew to be so powerfully present.

I feel it essential to the divine mystery of sisterhood to experience intense community life early on. It was then, in the very beginning of my religious life, somewhere and somehow in the constant togetherness, that those seeds of sisterhood stirring within were fertilized and nourished. I found lifelong friends and came to trust and treasure such togetherness as part of the mystery of life in religious community, as part of the mixing of sisterly ingredients in that great community cauldron, creating inner connections that would hold and bind us together for years to come. So holy is this kind of togetherness, this perpetual need of women to get together with other women, that almost all nuns build their community life around such sisterhood.

While in the beginning the constant physical togetherness, the intense experience of living in large groups, most clearly defined and created community life, it didn't take long to find out that physical proximity does not create community.

Whatever unites and holds us together is far more interior, far more a matter of the spirit, than that of regulated forms of community life or preferred kinds of community behavior. Depending upon the quality of life present among those living together, depending upon the depth of spirit that binds us together, religious communities, very much like families, can be just as dysfunctional, abusive and destructive as they can be life-giving, loving, and supportive. While I've tasted both in my years of communal living, it's by far the precious memory of the latter that lingers and heartens still.

Little by little over the years, it became more and more clear that those enduring bonds of trust, loyalty, and friendship are what create, nourish, and sustain community life. Affectionate attachment to, and profound solidarity with one another generates the divine energy with which community is built. Building community always was and always will be more a matter of heart and soul, more a matter of shared beliefs and bonds of friendship than of regulated or mandatory togetherness. As a result, it is not unusual to see sisters creating community life around their work, their mission, their ministry, and with those who share their vision of sisterhood, with those who can offer the kind of soulful friendship and solidarity upon which such sisterhood is built.

While some sisters still find such heartfelt support in traditional convents, others find the same in more free-form kinds of community life. Some live in ordinary neighborhood houses with one or two others, perhaps even with friends or family. Others live alone in small apartments, and gather together regularly with those who share their more solitary, independent vision of religious community. While such free-form, all-inclusive community life may look radically different from the life nuns traditionally live, such communities also bear witness, I believe, to that experienced by Jesus.

According to the Gospel of Matthew, someone interrupted Jesus asking him to leave what he was doing because his mother and brothers were there and wished to speak to him. Extending his hand toward the disciples, toward those followers with whom he was speaking, he said, "These are my mother and my brothers. Whoever seeks the will of God is brother and sister and mother to me"

(Mt. 12:46-50). Such is the community life that attracted and called me in the beginning, that gathering of random singlehearted seekers. Such is the community life that still calls me, and such it is, I find, that most attracts and invites other seekers to follow.

So important are the calls to friendship, solidarity, and community, that from the very beginning of religious life those experiences became sanctified in a consecrated vow, a promise made to God and one another forever, a promise we traditionally revered as equality and lived as poverty.

In the beginning of my religious life, poverty in the convent was everything I imagined it to be. We had very little. With the exception of our habits, a few clandestine personal treasures from former lives, some religious books and accessories, we had nothing. Not that I had a lot before entering the convent, but this was a kind of nothing I had never experienced. No TV, no stereo, no radio, no newspaper, no magazines, no phone, no fridge, no books other than religious ones, no leisurely bubble baths, and during Advent and Lent, no mail. On top of all that, for the first three years, all incoming and outgoing mail was censored, read by superiors. Often we received only the first and last pages of the letters sent by family and friends, the rationale being that if they had anything important to say, they would certainly say it in the first and last page. The more practical reason, we were told, was that the superior and her assistant didn't have the time to read pages and pages of letters written to the fifty of us. Whatever the reason, we were, in effect, cut off from all the ways we knew to keep in touch with former lives and loves.

For months I felt poverty stricken and deprived, but after the initial shock wore off, I found, much to my surprise, that I rather liked the little nothing feeling and the mysterious kinds of free time and space that accompanied it. The communal experience of poverty also offered comfort. We all had equal amounts of nothing. All of us new nuns were unplugged from our former life supports at the same time, bringing us all face to face with our ability or inability to find ingenious ways to survive the boredom and pain of withdrawal.

For starters, we all rather quickly learned to be unusually self-entertaining since we were our only source of entertainment. Talent shows were big, and theme parties would be planned months in advance. Some of the funniest, most heartwarming memories I have are of those years of having absolutely nothing but ourselves, and virtually all the time in the world. Even then, there was a kind of divine madness in the things we did. Even now a kind of surreal memory lingers of some such precious moments. One is the Christmas Day Talent Show, the first Christmas away from home for many of us, and the protest song one sister wrote (against the "No Razor" rule) and sang to the tune of "Let It Snow":

> "O the hair on our legs is frightful.
> And a razor would be delightful,
> But since it doesn't show,
> Let it grow! Let it grow! Let it grow!"

Or the poem another wrote and recited, entitled "The Sunbeam," written in protest against the one perfect postulant in the group who shot the good behavior curve for the rest of us.

The Sunbeam

She was a sunbeam, all sparkling and
   bright,
shedding her rays, from left and from
   right.
She was a sunbeam, with zeal unabated.
She was a sunbeam, and, boy, was she
   hated.

Part of me is still that easily entertained; I still nearly laugh to tears every time I remember that first Christmas in the convent when the fifty of us were left with nothing but our own resources.

Another fine feature of vowing poverty, of living a simple life, is found in how divinely poverty frees sisters from preoccupation with money and how inordinately important money is to the rest of the world. In the communal world of nuns, all we earn traditionally goes into a common fund from which each sister receives what she needs. The pure joy of treating each other equally clearly arises when everyone has what they need with some left over for giving away. In some religious communities, like Secular Institutes, or the Sisters for Christian Community, sisters are self-supporting, tax paying, and financially independent, while still remaining committed to supporting those members in need of financial assistance. Whether in or out of the convent, the best and most socially responsible consequence of vowing some degree of poverty, some degree of sharing resources, lies in having just enough left over to offer the kind of hospitality and assistance to others called for by our Christian commitment.

Regardless of how different poverty among nuns may look today from its austere beginnings, what really matters is sharing what we have with the very least among us, thereby preserving the divine mystery of equality, solidarity, and community. Poverty always was and always will be an inner vow of hospitality to all in need. Because the vow nuns make to share personal and financial resources extends the bonds of their sisterhood permanently to those in need, most nuns build their personal and communal lives around some degree of poverty and some significant measure of sharing with the very least among us, both inside and outside of the vowed sisterhood.

In looking back now over the past thirtyplus years, I see more clearly how friendship, solidarity, and community were the first mysteries that attracted and called me to the sisterhood of nuns. I also see how the soul of sisterhood, which holds sacred a woman's need to get together with other women, also holds as equally sacred a woman's need for solitude. Just as sisterhood calls all nuns to a life of solitude, so too does it call us to find a room of our own; to enter to taste and see how divine, how holy, and how sweet sisterhood is to all who follow the soulful call into solitude.

THREE

Solitude

Just as the call to sisterhood makes holy a woman's need to gather with other women, so too does the call to solitude make holy a woman's need to be alone for awhile, her need for a room of her own, and for regular time to spend there. Nothing is more essential to a woman's experience of divine life than preserving, protecting, and exalting her right to regular solitary periods.

Since the very beginning of religious life, solitude appeared as the sweetest, dearest, and probably the most personal call nuns heard as the heartfelt soul of the sisterhood as lived in religious communities. The call to solitude shapes our lives as nuns in ways different from most, very specific and celibate ways that protect as divine this sisterhood, this sacred need for women to be alone, as well as the sacred need for women to be together.

For me, the call to solitude became far clearer after I entered the convent. For eighteen years I lived with two sisters, two brothers, my parents, oftentimes one grandmother, a variety of pets, and no rooms of our own. If there was a call to solitude in the beginning, it never got a fair chance to be heard. In our house, peace and quiet was something you found only before sunrise. I remember my mother almost always waking before dawn. As for me, background noise was my constant companion, even my greatest comfort, as I remember always falling asleep and waking up to the music of either radio or stereo. Solitude and I were near complete strangers, but when we met my very first day in the convent, it felt like love at first sight.

Part of my immediate fascination and enchantment with solitude lie with the fact that when I entered the convent on September 13,

1964, the very first thing I was given by my sisters was literally a room of my own; a small, plain, single room, with desk, closet, sink, bookcase, bed, and window. I was told to enter the room, remove my worldly clothes, place them in the brown paper bag left on the bed, put on the habit and veil which hung in the closet, and when ready, join the other forty-nine new sisters down in the sewing room. The fact that I hated to sew no longer mattered, as I found myself stitching tiny little white cloth tags numbered 1053 on all my clothes, alerting both the convent laundry and me that those clothes were mine.

In the beginning, I ended up doing a lot of things I had always hated—waking at 5:00 a.m., making my bed every morning, keeping quiet nearly all day and night, eating liver, turning lights out at 9:00 p.m. None of it mattered much except waking at 5:00 a.m. Regardless of what happened during the day, in the end I could always go to my room, close the door, and take refuge in solitary splendor. At the end of every day, solitude called me to that sacred time and holy space where I could feel and think and do whatever I wanted. For that reason alone having a room of my own appeared as an amazing and saving grace. I met solitude in that room for the very first time and time after time since then. Even now I live in solitude in two rooms of my own, one in which to work and play, and one in which to sleep and pray.

One of the biggest shocks and adjustments for me in the beginning of my religious life was not being able to talk whenever I wanted. All day, every day, there was a general rule of silence in the convent. We could not talk to one another, could not bother one another unless it was absolutely necessary.

After the initial shock of not being able to talk wore off, after I learned how to communicate without talking, I began not minding the general rule of silence, the community effort to keep all fifty of us new nuns undisturbed all day by pesky distractions. For me, protection of a woman's right to solitude—a peace and quiet so unlike the rest of the world—was one of the religious life's finest features. As the old rule book wisely noted, "Conversational powers are no common gift, especially among women meeting daily in the same circle." I suppose the founding sisters thought that since we all did everything together at the same time, day after day, what else was there to say?

Even more important, though, the general silence created an atmosphere which freed us to focus, to concentrate, and to do whatever the day set before us, whether it be study, work, pray, or play. I believe the somewhat excessive need for solitude I now know came from all those days of routine silence, free from distraction and charged with all the singlehearted intensity necessary to enter solitude. Ordinary, everyday silence was my constant, oftentimes irritating companion in the beginning, and it was in such regular household silence that my life as a nun first began to unfold.

Talking during the day, or "breaking silence," was always judged to be a common sisterly fault in need of correcting. But at night, a profound and serious emphasis was given to what was called "The Great Silence," which according to the nun's rule book, was to be "especially observed." Breaking The Great Silence was judged as nearly unforgivable, and could even be cause, we were told, for dismissal. Even so, at first keeping quiet at night almost killed me and nearly led me to explode on occasion.

At first, I concluded that The Great Silence rule was really a gag order, made up to keep us from complaining at the end of the day when all of us were tired, and some of us sick and tired. My mother tells me that even as an infant I became more animated at night, so much so that it usually took a car ride around the block several times to put me to sleep. The simple fact that I'd been a night person since birth provided some explanation for the difficulty I experienced keeping seriously still and quiet at night. This was compounded by not having nearly enough time to say all that I wanted to say to my friends about what happened or didn't happen that day.

While most of my sisters fell soundly asleep moments after "Lights Out," no matter how tired I was, I often felt wide awake, just as though some of my lights went on at the same time the room lights went off. Darkness, silence, and solitude all of a sudden replaced radio and stereo in rocking me to sleep each night. Surprisingly and mysteriously, in time they became a great and divine comfort. Little by little, I most easily and naturally entered into solitude at night. And at night I began writing like

I never did before, sitting in the dark on the windowsill, writing by the glow of the streetlight.

Almost every night I wrote as though some from inner necessity, as though I could not, would not, rest and sleep until I had done so. I wrote long letters to family and friends that were rarely ever sent, clandestine notes to sisters that were passed on the next day, telling them everything I wanted to but never got a chance to say, and funny poems and stories that I illustrated and gave away as presents.

I still know the mysterious something about night that just begs for The Great Silence. There's something about all the darkness that quiets down the outside world and strangely brings us closer to ourselves, to how we really feel, to what we really think, in ways that are nowhere near as clear during the day. After years of writing every night I came to recognize the call to solitude and the call to write as those of The Great Silence and the Holy Spirit which abides therein. I also now recognize the clarity of both calls as a divine result of my not being able to talk whenever I wanted.

Part of the reason it still feels so normal, ordinary, and necessary for me to enter into solitude, particularly at the end of the day, is because everything about our early days as nuns prepared us, focused us, and disposed us to just that. Every day was filled with matters religious, thereby cultivating and nourishing what I now experience as a magnificent obsession with all things mysterious, all things extraordinary, all things divine. The only reading allowed us was *lectio divina,* spiritual reading, and even now, when for years I've been free to read whatever and whenever I want, my heartfelt preference is still for *lectio divina*—for books on God, rituals, the inner life, eastern and western mysticism, biographies and autobiographies of extraordinary people. So intense is my need for *lectio divina* that it has left me with my two rooms overflowing with such books.

The purpose of a somewhat austere novitiate experience, we were told, was to form our minds and souls as sisters through prayer and study. For the first three years, most of the college classes we took introduced and engaged us in the study of theology and philosophy, for me the most divine of the liberal arts. The subjects we pursued almost exclusively included the Old Testament—in particular the Prophets and the Psalms—the New Testament, the sacraments, theologies of God and Mary, the mystics, church history, community history, and the vows. Later we encountered a personal favorite, the mystics. Even now, when I'm free to study whatever and whenever I want, my heartfelt preference is still for those subjects which connect me to the world of religious life, the workings of the spiritual life, the mysterious world within where all manner of inspiration, imagination, insight, even miracles and healings occur.

Furthermore, if we weren't studying the divine arts, or engaged in *lectio divina,* we were praying, either communally or privately. Learning those meditative disciplines of the soul enabled us to tune out distractions, shift us from the outer to the inner world, alter our consciousness, and put us in touch with the gods. At least four times a day we gathered for communal prayer. And other "free time" was set aside for private prayer, the kind of time and prayer I loved most because of its sweet call to step apart and enter into solitude.

Oddly enough, free time and free space were hard to find in my first years in religious life. There wasn't the time for solitude in the convent that you'd think there'd be. Time together far out-weighed our time alone. Ordinary days were so closely and constantly scheduled with communal activities that pure solitude became a many-splen-dored thing. But even though time alone felt at a premium, I found that the otherworld of sister-hood clearly and consistently offered, even made mandatory, sufficient time and space necessary to enter into solitude. Never does religious life regard solitude as a particularly reprehensible waste of time and energy, a twisted form of passivity, or a pathological kind of narcissism. Nuns behold soli-tude not as the lot of the lonely, but always as their most divine sister, constant companion and advi-sor. Never as an absence of energy or action, but rather a boon of inner activity, of inner seeing, in-ner hearing, inner feeling, and inner knowing. Rarely is solitude experienced as a sterile place of boredom or melancholy. Even when it is, solitude remains a holy of holies wherein the mysteries of life and death are revealed, as is the face of God, the self made in the image and likeness of God, our very best self which does not harden, shatter, or break when incomprehensible things happen.

At first, when my capacity for keeping still lasted no more than ten or fifteen minutes, I spent practically all of my solitary free time outside the convent walking, rather than inside the chapel praying. Because the first few formative years were mostly cloistered, the area in which we could walk was generally restricted to the back of the campus we shared with Saint Mary's College which was owned and operated by the community. Such restrictions prevented us from socializing with the college students, another cause for dismissal. In particular, the only area in which we could lawfully walk was the convent cemetery, the burial ground for all the Sisters of the Holy Cross who had died since the community was founded in 1841.

Any creeps that death and cemeteries gave me before entering the convent quickly disappeared my second day when I attended three funeral Masses and three processions to the cemetery for three burials of nuns who died before I even arrived. But even then, like now, funerals were oddly and surprisingly a glorious affair, with what then seemed like hundreds of us accompanying our dead sister to the community burial ground where she would lie to rest with all of the other sisters who went before her. Even now, as then, the community chants the hymn, *In Paradisum,* which called on all the angels to conduct the deceased sister into Paradise. From that day on, the cemetery felt far more like a holy resting place for sisterly spirits than the creepy abode of the dead. From that day on I found it a place of eternal rest for my oftentimes restless spirit.

Whenever I couldn't keep still, whenever I felt far too antsy to enter into solitude, I took my restlessness outside and walked the cemetery, paced back and forth, up and down those rows of white stone crosses, reading all the nuns' names, aloud or to myself, like some kind of litany of the saints. Afterwards I did the same with their real names, their family names engraved on the back. The earliest sisters, I found, had the most unusual names, like Sister Five Wounds, whose family name was Mahoney. I called her "Five Wounds Mahoney," what I imagined her sister-friends calling her.

I also remember finding Sister Mary Circumcision, wondering first, if she died of embarrassment when she got her name, and second, what her sister-friends called her. One old nun who knew her told me they called her "Cirky" for short. Whatever made my spirit restless in the beginning was almost always soothed and calmed down by my constant walking, up and down those rows of white stone crosses in the nuns' cemetery, as well as by all those restful and peaceful sisterly spirits who always mysteriously assured me that somehow, "It will be resolved by walking." Oddly enough, it always was, and still is, whenever I go back to visit my sisters resting there in peace.

The very first thing I loved about solitude, the very first of its calls I heard was the call to "free space," time and space unoccupied with any other activity. There was no expectation other than listening and following the still, small inner voice, that Holy Spirit; following our divine intuition wherever it goes, even if it seems to go nowhere. Sometimes solitude becomes a matter of just being there and doing nothing, being there and abiding, reflecting on whatever the day put before us and waiting for some sense to be made of it all.

I treasured such solitary free time and free space far more than I did communal time. Such solitude always let me loose to tend to all the creative and playful spirits stirring within, as well as the disturbing, bewildering, and restless spirits which oftentimes accompanied them. As soon as I was alone, as soon as I was given free time and free space, as soon as I learned to stop fooling around and keep still, I found myself quite easily passing over into that other world. I was always eager to do so because of all the mysterious, insightful, humorous, creative, and divine life I found there.

Once given the free time and free space to be alone I never knew for sure where such intentional solitude would call me. I still don't. At first, I remember being called by solitude into what I came to experience as prayer, as meditation, as being called into my most soulful self where all kinds of learning from experience occurs. I fed solitude the days of my life, the stuff of my days and how I felt about them. In doing so, I also found myself listening for that still, small voice, the voice of God which called me. I listened and waited to hear what the Spirit had to say about my burning questions, my whining complaints, my strange experiences, my heartfelt hopes, and my unspoken prayers. I waited to hear what my soul, what my spirit had to say about this strange new life, listening for what counsel it would offer in response. Meditation and prayer became an inner consultation, a way of getting in touch with that inner voice. It became a way of begging for some explanation, for some understanding of what I had gotten myself into, of what was happening to me and why.

Whenever I meet with something clearly beyond my understanding, it always feels good to enter into solitude. Only there can I be most attentive to the mystery behind what happens and to the divine wisdom that such mysteries offer. I almost always find solitude the bearer extraordinaire of such divine wisdom, a comfort and a home for me wherever I am. I find it a permanent home from which I usually emerge refreshed and comforted by some vague knowledge of a next step—some better, clearer understanding of what's going on, of what's happening to me, and what I need to do next.

The prayerful activity that takes place in intentional solitude is, I find, unlike any other and is never a waste of time. On the contrary, not only does it bear divine comfort in all kinds of soulful suffering, but it also mysteriously prevents bitterness and the tendency I have when weary to whine and blame. Such soulful solitude almost always refreshes fatigue and relieves that weariness, provides surprising insight, endurance, and self-knowledge. Even the instinct and intuition about what's right and true becomes sharper in prayer. It reveals bits and pieces of life's most incomprehensible mysteries with a fresh, unique kind of humor unlike that I find anywhere else.

Whenever solitude calls me to prayer, whenever I follow my disturbing, restless, and puzzled spirits to their God and my God, I almost always find myself lifted up and carried through by them. Such prayerful solitude almost always makes it possible for me to continue on my way, regardless of what critics say, with the heartfelt conviction that it is divinely well worth my while to do so. While being called by solitude to contemplative prayer remains a call I hear in the sisterhood of religious life that I do not hear quite as clearly anywhere else in this world, the call to such solitary prayer is only half the truth of the matter. Without fail, nearly every time it happens, nearly every time I come into contact with God in that way, I almost always emerge hearing a clear call to create, in particular to write, to make something of what I heard and found there in solitude's prayer. Entering into such a solitary, soulful, and prayerful place, nearly always mysteriously wakens, moves, and induces that image of God we find in prayer to rise, to shine, and to make itself known.

Even before I entered the convent, I had always been attracted to the more creative and playful parts of grade school and high school activities, like making banners and signs for special events, painting scenery and sets for school plays, acting the female lead role in the Senior Class Play, *Harvey* (a play about an 8-foot imaginary rabbit), and simultaneously falling in love with everything imaginative and creative about the world of play and theater. But very much like the call to solitude and prayer, I heard the call to create far more clearly after I entered the convent.

Once in the convent, all of those creative activities I engaged in before were strongly encouraged, even sometimes made mandatory. We designed and sewed banners for liturgical celebrations, made table decorations for feast days, as well as scenery and sets for plays, skits, and talent shows done for special occasions. Saturday afternoons appear in my memory as arts and crafts time, later referred to by some of us as "arts and craps" because of all the things we made and gave to one another—rocks painted with "Love," "Peace," and "Joy," twig crosses, pressed leaves and flowers—things that were objects of some profound meaning at the time given.

Yet even more playful and engaging than making *chatchkis* in the arts and crafts room, was the call to write which I began to hear more and more frequently, more and more clearly. Rather than doing the arts and crafts, I usually preferred to be sitting under some big, old tree in the cemetery with paper and pencil, writing whatever. Such clear, pure impulses to create, in particular to write, almost always came after some period of prayerful solitude. I know now, far more so than I ever did in the beginning, that something creative usually happens in those solitary times, something entirely mysterious that nearly always leaves me wanting to do something, to make something, to work, to write like I never did before.

One of the most frequent questions I am asked is, "What do you write?" What do I write when solitude calls me? For some people writing is such a mysterious work that imagining doing so for a living becomes nearly impossible. For me, imagining not doing so has become just as impossible. Journals, letters, and books are what I write. And over the years each has become more of what I knew them to be in the beginning—simple and soulful sacraments of solitude.

I believe journal writing was the first call I heard, over thirty years ago, in the dark, on the windowsill, working by the glow of the campus streetlight, often to the sound of birds and crickets. Just as I did then, I still write mostly at night, near an open window, by the glow of a night-light. Only now I most often write to the sound of traffic, sirens, car alarms, and barking dogs. As a nun, I naturally spend a lot of time alone thinking about where life calls me and how well to respond. And as a writer I spend a lot of time keeping a journal of what I think and feel, of where the days take me, and what I find along the way.

For those who ask how to begin journal writing, I always suggest doing so with what you want to remember about each day and what you want to forget. Include the best and the worst of each day. Found in my daily journal are dreams I remember, books I'm reading, fortunes from cookies, movies I've seen, readings from runes, meals I loved, ticket stubs and playbills. Whatever sets one day apart from all the others ends up in the journal when day is done. Whatever swims through the stream of my consciousness also finds some place in its pages.

Far more than simply being a very good consciousness-raising, warm-up exercise for me as a writer, keeping a journal has also become a very good spiritual exercise for me as a nun. Because of its solitary nature, journal-writing naturally draws us into the otherworld of contemplative activity—inner seeing, inner hearing, inner feeling, and inner knowing, a world wherein all manner of darkness and light are found, as is that indestructible seed from which all rebirth comes. The solitary call I hear to write almost always comes from that contemplative world of inner activity, and always sounds like that of a dear old friend, of that Holy Spirit that's been calling on me for years. As such, journal-writing has become more a sacrament of my daily solitude, a place for the Word, an ordinary, everyday spiritual exercise that in the end grants extraordinary peace and insight.

For over twenty years, I've been writing daily, keeping a journal of the day's findings. The books of those findings, of which there are five to seven per year, then become the highlight of that monthly and annual new year retreat. One of the most common threads that weave our lives together as nuns is the need to retreat every now and then, to secure for ourselves sufficient time to be alone. The journals of the past month or year accompany me on every retreat as a kind of guide in examining my conscience. No retreat feels complete without that *lectio divina*, without reviewing prayerfully the best and worst parts of days past.

In the very beginning of my religious life, the first Sunday of every month was designated as the day to write letters. Three one-page (both sides) letters could be written then—one to parents, one to another nun, and one to a friend or other relative. In time, when restrictions on letter-writing were removed, every Sunday became letter-day, and every week I looked forward to Sunday's solitary call to write letters.

My love of letter-writing goes way back to those notes that teenage girls write incessantly and pass back and forth throughout the schoolday. Long before I ever discovered the call to letter-writing in the convent, I knew years of something similar in all the schoolgirl notes I wrote, passed, and received daily. Shoeboxes full. And based on what I know of my nieces now, schoolgirls still incessantly write and pass and receive notes all day long, as though in response to some primitive, heartfelt call for all women to write letters to one another and keep them in shoeboxes for years.

Very much the soul-sister to journal-writing, letters come from the same world of contemplative activity, and even appear as a kind of journal, only this time one written to others. Because of their soul-to-soul sacramental nature, letters seem to bear a mysteriously heartfelt power that somehow makes the sender present. The best part of any given day for me is always the arrival of a good long letter from a dear old friend. And the best part of any given Sunday is still spending the day writing good long letters to dear old friends, all the while feeling them present in doing so.

Letters always seem mysterious to me in the way they have of putting writers in touch with one another. People I've never met before become unforgettable in a letter. And the annual letters from those I've known for years become a constant treasure. Known or unknown, the pile of answered letters is always a permanent part of any time I secure for solitude, particularly on Sundays. Just as solitude calls me daily to journal-writing, so too does solitude call me regularly to letter-writing.

Of all the solitary calls I hear to create, writing books is clearly the one that still takes me most by surprise. While making little books for friends was always a favorite pastime, the call to give my life over to writing books always seemed way beyond anything I ever would or could do. Slowly but surely, however, I ended up giving more and more of my life over to writing. Now I would do no other work if I could. More and more frequently, book-writing draws me most deeply into the otherworld of contemplative activity, becoming just as much a sacrament of my solitude as are my journal and letter-writing.

Regardless of how painful writing may appear to be, the call to raise something, to make something out of what almost always feels like nothing, is in itself, an unpredictable, contingency-prone process. The Book of Genesis, as well as most myths of creation, suggest that even God prayed before creating the universe. Before the call to create, before creation takes place, there is that "hovering over a formless void" that God does, that staring at the vast white canvas or blank page, that egg on which the Deity broods and provides life-giving warmth. It's that contemplative, meditative concentration, that looking and gazing intensely into the utterly blank, unknown depths of the soul, which mysteriously brings forth some new creation from those deep dark waters.

The call to create often feels as though it rises from a deep, divine breath of God, like a muse with a message. We the creator, the artist, the writer, have only the bright idea of giving body and blood to that Holy Spirit, of putting that divine life, that oftentimes playful and amusing, but sometimes disturbing message, into words, paint, clay, music, or some other mysterious medium.

For the one who emerges from such hovering, brooding, contemplative activity, as well as for the beholder, the created object somehow comes alive at times and speaks to us in return. In some mysterious way it moves us, disturbs us, delights us, inspires us, touches something altogether divine in us that also wakens and comes to life, the more profoundly and universally a creative work "speaks" the more profoundly and universally it comes to be recognized as timeless, as a work of art.

In that pure-as-prayer way, the call to create becomes a profound religious experience. Every true artist I know speaks of a divine spark of inspiration that catches fire and moves us to create; a process that remains far more a mystery and miracle of sorts than a personal possession or a singular achievement. I know now, far more clearly than I ever knew before, that the call to pray and the call to create are both the sweet sisterly soulmates of solitude, and the sweet sisterly soulmates of all those who build their lives around solitude's creative call.

So profoundly important to the communal life of sisterhood is the call to solitude, to contemplative prayer, and to creative activity, that it's no wonder all nuns would vow to live a solitary life, a life of celibacy. And it's no wonder our solitary life, our celibate life, is what most distinguishes us and sets us apart in this world as insanely different, just as it has done in all forms of religious life throughout history. Way before I ever knew anything about the celibacy, I was always mystified by how nuns weren't at all interested in being married, particularly in a world that still tends to value a woman by when and whom she marries. Not only did an unmarried lifestyle seem most appropriate and fitting for communal living, it also seemed most appropriate and fitting for preserving a certain freedom, a certain kind of availability expected of nuns. Because nuns were single, unmarried, and childless, there was a sense in which they belonged to everyone, a very real sense in which they became "sister" to all. To me that's the heart and soul of celibacy—the freedom to respond anytime, anywhere, and to anyone in need, just as one would do for one's own sister.

While most women I know hear some call to sisterhood, some call to solitude, and maybe even some call to a solitary life, most draw the line when it comes to living a celibate life. Most people still see celibacy as an unhealthy and bewildering life because most still see and understand celibacy as only meaning no sex. Just as marriage is far more a matter of something completely other and more divine than losing the freedom of the unwed, so too is sex. In the words of Gertrude Stein, sex is "a part of something of which the other parts are not sex at all." It's those purely sensual aspects of sex that celibacy reveres and preserves as holy; those heart-to-heart, soul-to-soul connections and commitments without which sex breeds an emotional madness far from divine. I have never understood or experienced celibacy as just meaning no sex, even though that's pretty much how my solitary life almost always ends up working itself out. And never, ever do I feel tortured or about to explode from lack of sexual activity; on the contrary, I more often than not wallow in simple freedom and solitary splendor that no such emotional knots leaves me.

For me, the celibate part of my solitary life has always been far more a matter of freedom to go where and when the spirit calls than it ever is the lonely consequence of no marriage, no children, no lover, and no sex. The heartfelt matter of celibacy clearly comes from the heartfelt matter of the life-long friendship, companionship, emotional satisfaction, and enduring love that sisterhood and community life can offer. While vowing poverty teaches nuns how to treat one another with divine equality, vowing celibacy teaches us how to love one another just the same. More than anything else, the call to celibacy is a call to love one another so intimately and so profoundly that we always encourage and always provide one another with enough solitude in all the togetherness, to tend to the divinity we bear within, and to allow always for reflective living and creative, contemplative activity. Such is the heart and soul of sisterhood in religious life.

Even though in many ways I now look and live like anyone else, it's the solitary and celibate way I choose to live and love that I find clearly distinguishes me as different, even from other women who also hear a call to sisterhood and solitude. Most women imagine such celibate independence as too hard and lonely to bear, too impossible, too unhealthy, and too unnecessary to even consider seriously. For some strange, mysterious reason I do not.

I treasure such independence like a pearl of great price, like a gift from the otherworld that gives nuns a mysterious edge, a counter-cultural dimension. More than any other part of life in community, it's the divinely mad and celibate relationships we have that makes us a poor fit in a world gone mad with a dimension of sex too often not "part of something of which other parts are not sex at all."

More than anything else, the call to a solitary, celibate life, has far more to do with revering as holy and preserving as sacred our distinctive sisterly and communal lifestyle than it ever has to do with simply not having sex. Since the very beginning of religious life, solitude and celibacy have always abided as the heartfelt soul of sisterhood, as well as the heartfelt love of the sister. Because of that ancient, mysterious, and holy tradition of preserving the divine independence of the feminine spirit, the divine interdependence of the communal spirit, and the divine love of the solitary spirit, most nuns continue to build their lives around such lovingly celibate relationships. In doing so, the sisterhood promises forever to nourish those holy spirits which protect solitude's call to free space, to contemplative prayer, and to creative work, to making something out of what we hear and find there in such solitary prayer, to putting all of the divine, loving energy to work.

FOUR

Work

One of the first things I noticed about nuns was how they were all called to some kind of work, both inside and outside of the convent, and how they didn't retire from doing so until they got exceptionally old, seriously sick, or died. Nuns always worked long after the school day ended, even on Saturdays and holidays (but never on a Sunday or holy days), and often enlisted student help with classroom or church cleaning, decorating bulletin boards, and correcting papers. In grade school, I loved volunteering for such after-school work, mostly because of the little religious rewards we received for doing so. My favorite was a fountain pen in which a statue of the Blessed Mother floated up and down on a cloud whenever I held the pen up during spelling tests, then put it down to write.

In the 1950s and '60s, nuns were the only women I knew who worked outside of the home. They were the only women I knew who weren't wives, mothers, and grandmothers. They were also the only women I knew who had what this world calls a "real job." More importantly, the nuns I knew worked as though they were women with a mission, women for whom work was far more than a way to be self-supporting (which it rarely was), and far more than the path to fame and fortune (which it never was). The work nuns did was seen as "God's work," and the manner in which they devoted themselves to such work seemed to demand a certain singleheartedness, a certain exclusivity which their solitary, celibate life supported and nourished.

Just as nuns revered as holy a woman's need for sisterhood and solitude, so too did they revere a woman's need to work as a divine right. For nuns, all work is God's work. Even the most mundane, hidden, and ordinary kinds of tasks were perceived as one of the most natural ways for women to experience divine life, although sometimes I wondered if nuns just said that in order to make naturally unpleasant tasks seem more bearable.

Nuns aren't the only ones who regard a woman's need to work as a divine right, even though I believe they were probably among the first to do so. Social scientists now confirm the one bit of wisdom about women's mental health that nuns have known all along: work improves it. Researchers now report that women who've never worked outside the home tend to have the highest levels of depression. Single working women tend to fare a lot better than their unemployed married sisters, some of whom experience ". . . low self-esteem, feel least attractive, experience the most loneliness, and consider themselves least competent at everything, even child care."[1]

The call to work, both inside and outside of the home, was no stranger to me before or after I entered the convent, even though I always preferred to follow the call of my friends to come party and play. As far back as I can remember, the whole family was called to work in my grandfather's (later my father's) bakery. Even the youngest was given some tiny but nonetheless necessary task, as was everyone I knew who grew up with a family-owned business. In very much the same way, the religious community appeared to be a kind of family-owned and operated business, with all sisters called on right from the start to work in some way to help with the maintenance and upkeep of communal living.

A side of convent life—the more hidden, institutional side—once depended heavily on all nuns keeping the big buildings in which they lived, "convent clean." Floors were waxed almost weekly on hands and knees, then buffed with machines way bigger than most of us who operated them. And once a year, always during the hottest month of the summer and with no air conditioning, eight great big, wide flights of wooden stairs were sanded and varnished by hand. The sisters also helped care for the elderly sisters in the infirmary, particularly at mealtimes when hundreds of trays needed to be set and served, hundreds of pots, pans, and dishes washed and scrubbed.

The call to manual labor, to ordinary, everyday housework was and still is a call that nuns hear, even though diminishing numbers, aging members, and overworked sisters now have us relying heavily on others for assistance.

Nuns always referred to those household tasks as obediences (after the vow of the same name), just as they did all the other more church-related work they were called to do. With the poet Gerard Manley Hopkins, they believed the whole world was "charged with the grandeur of God." Every situation and all work was holy, a quite ordinary way for us to experience the presence of God. Consequently, we were taught to lay our hands on the ordinary things and common interests of life just as though they were indeed works of God, just as though those tiny insignificant-looking tasks were the most divine work we could possibly do.

So in the beginning of my religious life, pulling weeds from the cracks in the sidewalk, cleaning bird droppings off the picnic tables, and scrubbing toilets and shower stalls, were just as much my obedience, just as much God's will and work for me then, as teaching, counseling, and college administration were later, and writing is now. All the work we were given to do as nuns was understood and accepted as God's particular will and work for us. In the spirit of holy compliance we willingly or unwillingly went where we were sent, and did what we were called on to do. That's how obedience was lived even though I do recall scrubbing a particularly messy picnic table, cursing the birds, and calling to mind Teresa of Avila's comment to God after being thrown from her horse into a puddle of mud: "If this is how you treat your friends, it's no wonder you have so few."

When I first became aware of nuns, regardless of how ordinary the work was that they did, I always recognized such work as "God's work," and always saw nuns as God's workers. In some mysterious way they were related to God and endowed with an authority we were taught to obey without question. Whatever sister said and did was right. Rarely would we go home and complain about being unfairly reprimanded because we'd just get yelled at all over again by our parents and grandparents. Even so I don't remember the meanness of nuns that some now write and talk about, as much as I recall their extraordinary kindness to those who needed special attention. They showed an overall interest in and concern about what saddened us as well as what made us happy. Such everyday compassion and merciful authority set their work apart, distinguishing them more in my eyes as women with a mission, rather than simply spinsters with a career.

The nuns I knew hardly ever seemed motivated in their work by meanness, self-interest, or the desire to profit at our expense. Never did I feel manipulated, used, or abused by them, even though some would've been canned today for their whacking disciplinary practices, including the steel-edged ruler over my knuckles for poor penmanship. All whacking aside, most nuns I knew seemed motivated in their work by their singlehearted desire to care for the personal needs of those they taught, in particular those most in need of special attention. As they did so, we learned to care for one another just as they cared for us.

Regardless of what particular job nuns had, and regardless of some of their wacky disciplinary practices, the loving work of God really seemed to be their primary work, and the compassion of

Christ their true mission. Nuns were unlike anyone else I knew in that regard, and it was in that
loving regard that I most wanted to be like them,
most wanted to do the kind of work they did.

When I entered the convent at age eighteen,
and with the exception of my desire to "help people," I had no clear idea at all of the kind of work
I wanted to do, or felt called to do. But then again
neither do most eighteen year-olds. The self-
knowledge we have at that age rarely affords us
such clarity of insight. Teaching, nursing, and missionary work were the traditional jobs of most
nuns at that time. All of the above appealed to me
in some naive way, even though the smell of hospitals and the stories I heard of missionary life
made me feel faint.

For the first twenty-five years of my life as a
nun, I pretty much gladly did what I was called on
to do, and willingly went where I was sent. As a
college student in the mid-1960s, I taught art and
religion to sixth and eighth graders, and loved
every day of it. More than anything else, I enjoyed
the kinds of things we did together after school and
on weekends—visiting the old nuns in the convent

infirmary, gathering food and clothing for needy families, going away with small groups for weekend retreats, and directing class plays. As was true for me throughout all my years of schooling, I still found myself investing most of my time and energy in the kind of education and lifelong learning that went on outside of the classroom.

Because my extracurricular or co-curricular interests were always so strong, I chose Sociology as a major in college with the intent of doing social work afterwards, even though there were no nun social workers at that time. In 1969, the closest acceptable nun work to social work was high school counseling, which I was given as an obedience, along with teaching theology to junior girls and sociology to senior boys. Most of these boys were on the football team, and taught me far more about football than I'm sure they ever learned about Sociology. Even while I loved every day I did that work, I also found myself drawn more to counseling than teaching, and more to the activities we engaged in at night and on weekends than those which occurred in the classroom.

Slowly but surely, it became more and more clear I was singleheartedly called to the life and the learning that went on outside the classroom; to how students made decisions, solved problems, developed friendships, made commitments, and searched for God.

My tenure with high-school students ended after three years, the last of which was spent as Dean of Girls at Bishop Noll High School in Hammond, Indiana, the high school from which I graduated in 1964. Both my brothers still attended the school at the time (as did the brothers and sisters of my classmates).

This was the job in which I felt as though I had the sins of my past heaped upon me. It was the year Jane Fonda accepted the Oscar for *Klute,* unbuttoned to the waist and braless. The very next day twenty-some senior girls appeared dressed the same, claiming no technical violation of the dress code. I spent most of that day driving those students home to get dressed. If I remember correctly, it was then that I also began hearing the call to do some other kind of work, perhaps to go to graduate school to study mysticism.

The mid-1970s proved to be a turning point for me in discerning my particular call to work. During those years, I returned to writing again at the end of every day after rarely doing so for three years as though I had somehow lost my voice. In retrospect, it now appears as though the years of high school work silently but surely drove me into a strange kind of solitude, even to the point where I oddly began to think seriously about joining a contemplative community of nuns, even living as a hermit in the woods. For me it was a most strange turn of events, and one completely beyond my understanding. The only call I heard loudly and clearly was in the Gospel of Mark where Jesus says the disciples to "Come away to some lonely place all by yourself and rest awhile (Mark 6:31)."

I then went to graduate school at the University of Notre Dame to study Theology. I studied mysticism, in particular the fourteenth century English mystics (Julian of Norwich was and still is a personal favorite), and received a master's degree in 1972. It was then also that I received a call, a telephone call actually, to think about working in Campus Ministry at Saint Mary's College, the Catholic women's college owned and operated by the Sisters of the Holy Cross, as well as my alma mater, the Mother of my mind. Campus Ministry was new, replacing what was traditionally the Chaplain's Office, and the job seemed to offer the opportunity for the kind of work I knew and loved best: late-night educational programs and activities, volunteer services, counseling, small-group weekend retreats, and solitary living.

My work as a Campus Minister began a nearly twenty-year career in college administration at Saint Mary's. I lived alone in the residence halls with the students for over ten years, sitting up with them well into the night, listening to the best and worst of their days, as well as that of their love lives. Once again I enjoyed thoroughly every day that I did so.

The late-night hours were a natural for me, as was being part of the ordinary, everyday lives of the students with whom I lived. We did volunteer work together twice a week, planned small group liturgies, prayer groups, and parties. In doing so, we built a community that caused those bonds of sisterhood to form and last for life. Twenty years later I still hear from many of those women, still receive the annual Christmas cards with pictures of all their children and updates on their lives, and still see them face to face whenever the opportunity presents itself, just like *Chere Amies*.

Throughout all my years of living, working, praying and playing with college students, as Campus Minister, then Residence Hall Director, then Dean, I almost always found myself and felt myself called in two directions at the same time—called to be together with the students and my sisters and called to be alone. Slowly but surely, year after year, I found the call to solitude to increase in intensity, oftentimes leaving me bewildered over how best to respond.

I spent two summers discerning what to do about the mysterious, near constant call to solitude I still hear now. I spent one summer in Monroe, Michigan with the Immaculate Heart of Mary sisters at their House of Prayer, and one summer in Guelph, Ontario with the Jesuits for a 45-day silent retreat. It was then and there I started to hear—like I never heard before—the clarity of that inner voice which called me to be a nun in the very beginning, and now called me further to something more.

For years I remained haunted by the silent and solitary life of contemplative nuns, who I imagined baked bread, tended sheep, made art, and cultivated vineyards. I felt a particular affinity with Thomas Merton, who as a Trappist monk lived alone in a hermitage, wrote books, and died on my twenty-first birthday. The only thing I can think of that prevented me from joining a contemplative group was the instinct I have always had to abandon anything that separates me in any way from others, whether that be the way I dress, the way that I live, the work that I do, even what people call me. Even titles such as Sister or Doctor (as in Ph.D.) make me feel once or twice removed from people in a way that feels completely unnecessary.

It has always felt essential for me to maintain a level of normal existence in the world, some normal work life as a balance to the strange, intense, inner life I began to know. Work and solitude have been so joined together in me that it feels as though neither can survive, neither can be enjoyed fully, without the other. Solitude feels altogether empty without some ordinary kind of work and everyday work feels even emptier without solitude. As a matter of self-preservation, I still need both.

I'll never forget the dream I had in May 1976, somewhere in the middle of the forty-five-day, silent retreat, while I did the Ignatian Exercises. I was sitting in a restaurant with my retreat director, having dinner and discussing the need I felt to leave my work in Campus Ministry for an unknown something else. The name of the restaurant was "The Manner Is Ordinary," carved into a big, old wooden sign hanging out front. I remember nothing more than that. The following year I left my work as a Campus Minister to become a Residence Hall Director. In this position I became more of an older sister to the students, became more involved in their ordinary lives than I ever managed as Campus Minister. Whatever I was called to do with the rest of my life, whatever work I ended up doing, one mandate was clear: the manner must be ordinary.

Inside and out, the 1970s proved to be a turning point for the work I was called to do, as it did for a majority of women in religious communities at that time. Inner experiences and calls, as well as outward experiences and needs, joined to shape and influence my work life and my increasingly solitary life. Similar experiences and calls affected the lives of all nuns who welcomed with open minds and hearts the changes resulting from the papacy of John XXIII and the teachings of Vatican Council II.

Those were the years religious dress was modernized and sisters began opting for small group or solitary living. Some began pursuing more non-traditional work that utilized their particular skills, talents, and interests, even work that called them into worlds other than religious ones. Obedience became just as much a matter of listening to the voices within and without, as well as the voices of the community to which we were committed. Above all, sisters became increasingly committed to rebuilding their lives and work around the compassionate calls of the Gospel.

For nuns, obedience has always been a matter of where we go with our lives and what we choose to do with them, as well as whose voice we listen to in making decisions. In that regard, the call to solitude, the call to listen to our inner voice, always precedes the call to work and becomes the truest foundation for experiencing how divine work can be.

All of us, I believe, are moved by some pure instinct, by some divine call to live our lives in a certain way, even to do something only we can do, regardless of how ordinary and common it appears. There is this kind of psychic predisposition in us, I think, that by nature is turned toward the Divine, always motivating us to experience how divine life can be. In the center of our soul, in our heart of hearts, lies the secret of who we are. By listening closely for the secret to be revealed, we are led to what's right for us, and are given the strength and courage to obey.

In 1982, shortly after I began doctoral studies in college administration at New York University, another turning point appeared in my call to work, one which would take nearly seven years to make itself fully known. During those years, I realized the more deeply involved I became in student life at the college, and the more consumed I became by my work with the young women there, the more profoundly I experienced a call to solitude. I began to hear more clearly then, as I do now, the call to create that such solitude bears, in particular the call to write.

It was quite by accident, and altogether to my surprise, that my first book—a cookbook—was published, as well as my second and third for that matter. All were inspired by and written for the students with whom I lived and worked. At the time, neither I nor my sisters perceived writing as real work, as "God's work." It was a sort of secondary talent I had, almost like a hobby to be done in my spare time, or on vacation, but never a full-time job or a church-related ministry.

Even the college faculty (for whom writing and publication were requirements for promotion and tenure), struggled sometimes desperately to find time for research and writing. In very much the same way, I also struggled to find the time in my student-filled days as Dean to write the reports, letters, grants, and meeting minutes, not to mention a doctoral dissertation. My own writing, even my writing at the end of every day, got pushed into the slim, solitary margins of my life, mostly late at night after student life settled down, or in those rare times—like during Notre Dame football games—when practically all of the students were gone.

Most of my colleagues who wrote at that time tended their creative lives in similar solitary margins, which was always a source of comfort. Even now, everything about both this world and the more traditional convent world tends to discourage highly individual creative efforts. It's as though such efforts are by nature suspect because of their solitary origin, and consequently of their minimal potential benefit to society. Anything that solitary and individualistic tends to seem selfish, and of minimal benefit to the well-being of others, even though such creative work arises from the same solitary movement as does all soulful work which touches, moves, and changes the lives of those who hear it, see it, sense it, and know it.

I suppose, in an ironic sense, that the lack of support and approval is a blessing in disguise for those called to the more solitary works of art. It's far easier to maintain that critical eye and cutting edge of creative independence when such approval is lacking than it is when one is seduced by its favor and becomes blindly obedient to its expectations. Maybe that's why history shows us how so many artists and writers do their best and most brilliant work within an atmosphere of isolation, condescension, and loneliness. The real curse and tragedy of such disapproval, however, lies with all the unknown individuals who bear such divine creative potential that has no place or space in their lives. Eventually they end up depressed, mean, angry, self-serving, chronically fatigued, and maybe even seriously ill as a result. I count it as no small, random blessing that in 1989, inner experiences and calls, as well as sudden outward circumstances and needs, joined to change and shape my life and influence my work in ways far beyond anything I could have asked for or imagined.

In very much the same way that high school work in the early 1970s mysteriously and rather delightfully led me into the solitary life I now know and love as a nun, so too did college work lead me into the solitary work as a writer that I know and love as a nun. In 1989, I left my academic career of nearly twenty years, and shortly thereafter moved to New York City to phinally phinish my never-ending Ph.D. at New York University. I also intended to pursue the writing life and work I long felt called to do.

It still feels most essential to me now, just as it did in the very beginning of my call to work, to maintain some normal life in this world, some ordinary work life, some ordinary "day job" as a kind of necessary balance to the inordinately solitary life and work I now know. Ordinary work and extraordinary solitude are still so joined together in me that neither is as nearly divine without the other.

My life and work now as a nun have never been more ordinary, never been more extraordinary, and never felt more madly divine. By day, as my coworkers say, I "bring religion to retail" by helping an old friend and sister (but no longer a nun) manage her East Village (in New York City) toy store called ALPHABETS. I do very much of the same administrative work I loved doing as Dean, only in a non-academic, far more culturally rich and diverse environment. I still find enormous pleasure in the lives of those with whom I work (many of whom are college-age), along with the deliverymen, sales reps, neighborhood residents, fellow business owners, long-time customers whose children I watch grow, even the homeless who live and sleep outside the store. In one way or another, all somehow still call on me as they would their own sister, for support, counsel, fun, prayer, money, food, even a solitary place to stay for a day or two. All are neighbor, brother, and sister and community to me.

By night, I write and feel altogether at home doing so in a city overflowing with artists and writers, in a city that never sleeps. A psalmist reminds us it is at night that ". . .our heart instructs us"; it is at night that we hear more clearly those still, small, voices, and at night we can more clearly bring those divine images from the unseen world into being.

At night I write just as I did in the very beginning of my religious life by the light of a streetlight, in a Great Silence, long after "lights out." Only I do so now as long as the writing voice speaks, often well into the night, with no need to waken at dawn because few businesses in the neighborhood lift their gates before noon. By day, the manner of my work can hardly be more ordinary; by night the manner of my solitude can hardly be more extraordinary. All day long, and well into the night, the call to both has never felt more divine.

It seems strange to me that some in this world, and in religious life, still believe that nuns are most appropriately called and qualified to do only church-related or religious work. Even more than strange, it almost seems a sacrilege to demand that anyone should ignore or dismiss a heartfelt vocation in order to do something more acceptably religious in the eyes of this world. It is as if God is found only in church work and any other work is unfit for the presence of God or God's workers. I find it profoundly disheartening to think that maybe we've lost that magnificent sense we once had of all work being holy, of all work being God's work. Even ordinary tasks are mysterious ways in which the presence of God can be realized.

In the beginning of my religious life there was always that wonderful belief that the whole world was charged with the grandeur of God, and every person in every place, regardless of their appearance or lifestyle, was none other than Christ among us, none other than God-with-us. In the beginning, holy obedience always called us to those non-religious looking works, to those messy, menial tasks (like cleaning up bird droppings) with that truth in mind, lest we think that God wouldn't be caught dead doing some work or living in some neighborhoods. Sometimes I wonder if that's why women don't want to be nuns any more. Maybe we've become too exclusively religious in a way that alienates others and removes us from this world, so much so that religious life is no longer attractive.

Whatever the reason for the current alienation of affection contemporary women feel from the sisterhood of nuns, I do know how profoundly important it is for us to still do what there is a deep spiritual and emotional need for us to do—to vow some kind of holy obedience to what our heart loves most, to whatever moves us most profoundly and offers us peace.

Nuns have always built their lives around that most divine inner mystery by vowing obedience to God forever, by doing what the most Holy Spirit within asks. Only by prayerfully doing so with the help of our sisters can we ever be led to the path of God's particular work for us. Only then can we ever hope to taste, see, and experience the pure joy of how divine life can be, a joy not found separate or apart from this life, but in the fullness of it. Such holy obedience, I believe, is the source of our brilliance, the source of our experience of divine life, and the source of our madness. It is the wellspring of that call to live our lives in such an extraordinary, otherworldly way that in this world seems like madness.

1. Susan Faludi, *Backlash: The Undeclared War Against Women,* New York: Crown Publishers, Inc., 1991, 36-37.

FIVE

Madness

The sheer madness of my decision to become a nun was nowhere near as clear to me in 1964 as is my decision to remain a nun now. After thirty years I find myself more consciously attracted to living on the edge of society now than I even was then, living in that solitary margin where all things mysterious happen. I feel as though I live neither altogether in this world, nor altogether in that more inner world, but altogether in both, slipping back and forth wherever the days take me. In the end though, I always return to the solitary world within, to that otherworld of sisterhood in which I feel most at home at the end of the day.

Because most nuns live every day with the divine madness of having one foot in each world, it becomes important every now and then to make clear the ways in which we preserve, maintain, and revere as holy our marginality, our difference, our being a poor fit in a world where fitting in continues to mean far more than it ever should. Many of us may no longer look like nuns used to look, live the way nuns used to live, or do the kinds of church-related work that all nuns once did. Yet the heart of being a nun and the divine madness of the call remain the same. Even though some of us appear to look like everyone else, something about being a nun always has and always will stand in direct opposition to the age in which we live, always will rebel in non-violent ways against the status quo. The gate to the sisterhood of nuns remains just as narrow now as it always was and its way of life just as much an oddity, if not more so. Just as nuns revere the call to sisterhood solitude, and work as holy, so too we revere our oddness and our madness in this world as a divine call.

While I now pretty much work and live like any other solitary woman might, I still find myself paying an inordinate amount of attention to religious matters, to the mysterious workings of God within and without. As such I sometimes find myself a stranger in a strange land. I suppose any life that appears more solitary or contemplative, not to mention celibate, tends to be little appreciated in the western world. While a more religious culture—like that of India—may find nothing surprising or shocking about nuns and monks who devote their lives to an invisible God our world tends to view such religious commitment as odd, unprofitable, even wasteful.

Since the beginning of time probably, the things of God were always considered foolishness and madness. And as was true for me in the beginning, is now, and ever shall be true, the call to be a nun comes entirely from that divinely foolish world.

The call to madness I know is altogether the result of listening to the divine voices within and without, and gradually letting myself be led by the best. I know of no more divine way of life than the one in which I now live. I am quite certain now that if we never envision and trust ourselves as bearers of divine life, and never wholeheartedly believe in our eternal right to live in such happy-ever-after fulfillment, ". . .then we have betrayed and lost our soul, substituting for it a madness which leads to destruction, as our time demonstrates all too clearly."[1]

Perhaps the greatest and most mysterious source of our madness as nuns comes from how completely we vow to give ourselves over to being guided by the God within, the call of the Gospel, and the inspired voices of one another. An enormous wealth of wisdom is made available when women listen to God in that way, when they trust their divine instinct, even when they dare at times to appear odd, eccentric, or foolish. "If a fool would persist in her folly," William Blake once said, "she would become wise." Persisting in our unique folly as nuns holds great promise for seeking and finding the divine wisdom that makes sense of and gives moral content to the most bewildering experiences of life. For me, such wisdom always comes when least expected and always when I let myself be altogether guided by the God within.

Part of our madness as nuns also comes from the holy indifference we tend to have toward voices other than those of our Holy Spirit, scripture, and the discerning voices of one another. More than anyone else probably, nuns pay the least attention to what the secular world calls women to be and to do, and care the least about what it thinks of us. Some of the habits we wore (or still wear), and some of the names we bore (or still bear), attest to that fact quite clearly. Our standards of normality are so different from the rest of the world's, and are so closely identified with those of the Gospel, that we tend to have little or no regard whatsoever for what this world wants women to be.

As a result of this singlehearted attention to the mysterious workings of God in the world, a surprising independence emerges, bringing with it the inner strength every outcast needs to stand firm in the face of opposition and trust the only truth we know. Another part of our divine madness comes from the plain, rather obvious fact that we have little or no personal need for or dependence upon men to bring us happiness or security. Because women have always been pretty much born and raised to be dependent upon men for security, those who don't need or want to be are still treated as misfits or oddities. Even social scientists treat nuns and unmarried women as statistical deviants, indicating that we are not normal in the way that the world expects women to be normal.

As far back as I can remember, the celibate independence of nuns always seemed an oddity. Even now, independent women, celibate or not, still appear suspect of selfishness, of somehow living contrary to their "interdependent nature." Yet nothing can be further from the truth in my experience as a nun. The independence I found in sisterhood remains the sole, blessed source of any true religious experience of community I know. And some of the very best and most vital community-builders are those women, and those nuns, who appear inordinately independent in the eyes of some.

The most powerful and divinely mad part of our independence as nuns still lies with how profoundly it frees us to go where our most holy spirits call, and to do whatever those holy spirits ask of us. In particular, I find the spirits ask that we trust one another, love one another constantly from the heart, and abandon any tendency we have to judge, exclude, dominate, or disassociate from those who are not made in our own image and likeness. The call to be community-builders in an increasingly fragmented and mean-spirited society is clearly part of the divine madness I know as a nun, especially since our celibate independence makes such community-building possible.

While many tend to regard independence as a divisive force in community building, I find it quite the opposite. The independence I know creates a mysterious free space around us, a spiritual and emotional welcome mat for all to enter and make themselves at home. All are welcome. Most welcome are the very least among us, those this world shoves into its deepest, darkest, and coldest corners so as not to be seen or heard. In a world where people and nations continue to kill one another mindlessly in order to protect racial, cultural, even religious exclusivity, the madness of nuns serves as a reminder of those common human bonds that call all of us together in community.

Regardless of what we do as nuns, what we wear, or how we live, the singlehearted and passionate pursuit of justice always will be our mission, our one and only life work.

In looking back now over all thirty-plus years of my life as a nun, the call to madness has always been one of the strangest and most comforting calls I hear. I suppose it is crazy to think that a fairly intelligent woman would devote her entire adult life to some invisible God and what she wholeheartedly believes this invisible God asks of her. Even crazier still is the fact that every day I listen for the voice of that invisible God and follow the spirit wherever it goes.

More than any of the other voices I hear in this world, I pay attention to those inner voices, to the voices that call in the Gospels, and to the divine voices of my sisters, in and out of the convent. Hearing voices that few others hear has always been a sure sign of madness, and so it seems to be with me now. All the extraordinarily good things that have happened to me over the years clearly came from following those holy spirits, from walking through those clouds of unknowing, even doing those things I once feared most.

Crazier still is how indifferent I've grown, how holy and altogether indifferent most nuns I know have become, to what others think we should or shouldn't do. Over the years I've grown inordinately independent of what the secular world calls women to be and to do, both as a celibate woman in a couple's world and a solitary woman in the world of women's religious communities. Just as being single, celibate, and solitary appear to be sheer madness in this world of couples, lovers, and partners, so too does a solitary life appear odd in the world of religious communities. The call I hear to a solitary life as a nun, to the solitary work of writing, to the financially supportive work I do in retail, all seems crazy for a nun, altogether different from what a nun should look like or what a nun should be doing.

Yet the divinest sense of all, I believe lies in the madness of God's workers entering into every corner of this world, into every kind of work because the presence of God needs to be nurtured there as well.

Nearly every part of my life as a nun gives reason for someone to say, "You're crazy," and nearly every time I hear those words, I never dare dispute the claim. My greatest comfort always comes from knowing that because of the grace of God I am what I am. Because of that grace I am where I am today, doing the most unusual work I'm now called to do. I am altogether well-pleased with all the roads my life has traveled, as well as with all the unexpected turning points along the way. Everything around me, behind me, and before me seems just as mysterious and enchanting now as the voices and calls I heard to be a nun were in the very beginning. I cannot imagine a life richer than the one I know now. Nor can I envision being a nun in any other way than the solitary and ordinary manner in which I am now called to be. I still walk through those doors which offer the greatest opportunity to be and do my very best. And I still find myself living happily as a result.

Only time will tell if what we witness now is the final chapter in the history of Catholic nuns in this country, or if some new form of sisterhood is emerging from the cauldron of diversity we find in the different dress, works, and lifestyles among nuns today. Whether or not the sisterhood of nuns can survive as a significant force in making this world a holier and more peaceful place depends on the insight and courage of those who envision sisterhood for a new age. Only those who still hear the divine voice which called them in the very beginning can dream the dreams or see a vision for the future.

Even though the manner of being a nun has become, for some, so ordinary as to appear normal, at heart we as nuns remain just as different, just as otherworldly, and just as odd as we were when we looked that way. What really distinguished us then and now are the voices we choose to listen to and to let lead our lives, the community we feel called to build wherever we go, and the solitude we need as much as the air we breathe.

One thing remains most clear in the end. The God who called women to religious life has not lost interest in such sisterhood. The God who called women to sisterhood in the beginning still depends on women, perhaps more now than ever before, to make this earth a holier, healthier, and more peaceful place.

The calls of God to sisterhood—to solitude, to work, and to divine madness—are far clearer to me now than they ever were in the beginning, far dearer to me now than they ever were in the beginning, and far more madly divine than I ever imagined they could be.

Given the pure pleasure of friendship I now find in following the divine call to sisterhood, given the pure peace and comfort I now find in following the divine call to solitude, given the richness of life I now find in following the divine call to work, and given the pure delight I now find in following the divine call to madness, I cannot imagine why any woman wouldn't want to be a nun. Could it be Madness—this?

1. Carl Jung, *Mysterium Coniunctionis*, R.F.C. Hull, trans., Bollingen Series XX, Princeton, N.J.: Princeton University Press, 1970, 167.